my revision notes

Edexcel GCSE (9–1) History

WEIMAR AND NAZI GERMANY

1918–39

Steve Waugh

**HODDER
EDUCATION**
AN HACHETTE UK COMPANY

In order to ensure this resource offers high-quality support for the associated Pearson qualification, it has been through a review process by the awarding body. This process confirms that this resource fully covers the teaching and learning content of the specification or part of a specification at which it is aimed. It also confirms that it demonstrates an appropriate balance between the development of subject skills, knowledge and understanding, in addition to preparation for assessment.

Endorsement does not cover any guidance on assessment activities or processes (e.g. practice questions or advice on how to answer assessment questions), included in the resource nor does it prescribe any particular approach to the teaching or delivery of a related course.

While the publishers have made every attempt to ensure that advice on the qualification and its assessment is accurate, the official specification and associated assessment guidance materials are the only authoritative source of information and should always be referred to for definitive guidance. Pearson examiners have not contributed to any sections in this resource relevant to examination papers for which they have responsibility. Examiners will not use endorsed resources as a source of material for any assessment set by Pearson. Endorsement of a resource does not mean that the resource is required to achieve this Pearson qualification, nor does it mean that it is the only suitable material available to support the qualification, and any resource lists produced by the awarding body shall include this and other appropriate resources.

The Publishers would like to thank the following for permission to reproduce copyright material.

Photo credits: p11 INTERFOTO/Alamy Stock Photo; **p16** Munich Putsch, 1940 (oil on canvas), Schmitt, H. (fl.1940)/Private Collection/Peter Newark Pictures/Bridgeman Images; **p21** Punch Limited; **p33** Everett Collection Historical/Alamy Stock Photo; **pp37, 39** ullsteinbild/TopFoto; **p42** Fine Art Images/HIP/TopFoto.

Acknowledgements: mark schemes reproduced by kind permission of Pearson Education Ltd

Every effort has been made to trace all copyright holders, but if any have been inadvertently overlooked, the Publishers will be pleased to make the necessary arrangements at the first opportunity.

Although every effort has been made to ensure that website addresses are correct at time of going to press, Hodder Education cannot be held responsible for the content of any website mentioned in this book. It is sometimes possible to find a relocated web page by typing in the address of the home page for a website in the URL window of your browser.

Hachette UK's policy is to use papers that are natural, renewable and recyclable products and made from wood grown in sustainable forests. The logging and manufacturing processes are expected to conform to the environmental regulations of the country of origin.

Orders: please contact Bookpoint Ltd, 130 Milton Park, Abingdon, Oxon OX14 4SE.
Telephone: +44 (0)1235 827720. Fax: +44 (0)1235 400454. Email: education@bookpoint.co.uk
Lines are open from 9 a.m. to 5 p.m., Monday to Saturday, with a 24-hour message answering service.
You can also order through our website: www.hoddereducation.co.uk

ISBN: 978 1 5104 0327 7

© Steve Waugh 2017

First published in 2017 by
Hodder Education
An Hachette UK Company
Carmelite House, 50 Victoria Embankment
London EC4Y 0DZ

www.hoddereducation.co.uk

Impression number   10 9 8 7 6 5 4 3 2 1
Year   2021 2020 2019 2018 2017

Cover photo © World History Archive/Alamy
Illustrations by Gray Publishing
Produced and typeset in Bembo by Gray Publishing, Tunbridge Wells, Kent
Printed in Spain

A catalogue record for this title is available from the British Library.

How to get the most out of this book

This book will help you to revise for the modern depth study Weimar and Nazi Germany, 1918–39.

Use the revision planner on pages 2–3 to track your progress, topic by topic. Tick each box when you have:

1 revised and understood each topic

2 completed the activities

3 checked your answers online.

This book is organised into a series of double-page spreads which cover the specification's content. The left-hand page on each spread has the key content for each topic, and the right-hand page has one or two activities to help you with exam skills or to learn the knowledge you need. Answers to these activities can be found online at www.hoddereducation.co.uk/myrevisionnotes or by scanning the QR code on the book's back cover. Quick multiple-choice quizzes to test your knowledge of each topic can also be found on the website.

At the end of the book is an exam focus section (pages 38–46) which gives you guidance on how to answer each exam question type.

There are a variety of **activities** for you to complete related to the content on the left-hand page. Some are based on **exam-style questions** which aim to consolidate your revision and practise your exam skills. Others are **revision tasks** to make sure that you have understood every topic and to help you to record the key information about each topic.

Tick to track your progress as you revise each element of the key content.

Content for each topic is on the left-hand page.

Key terms and **Key individuals** are highlighted in the section colour the first time they appear, with an explanation in the margin nearby. As you work through this book, highlight other key ideas and add your own notes. Make this *your* book.

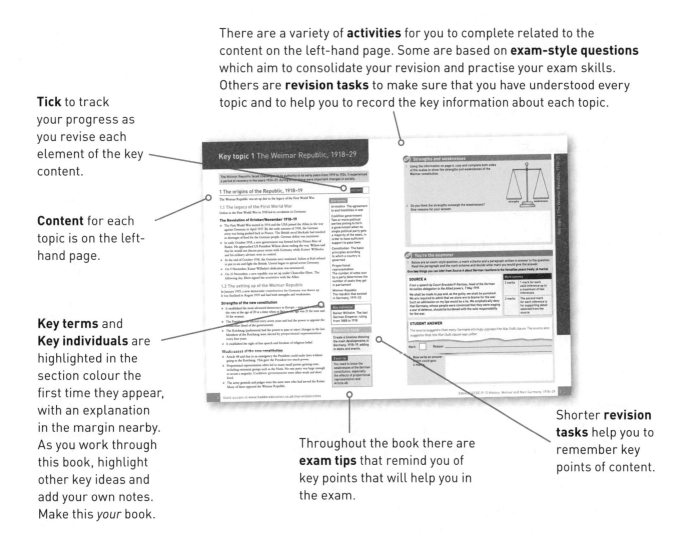

Throughout the book there are **exam tips** that remind you of key points that will help you in the exam.

Shorter **revision tasks** help you to remember key points of content.

Contents and revision planner

Key topic 4: Life in Nazi Germany, 1933–39

Exam focus

Question 1: Inference

Question 2: Causation

Question 3(a): Utility

Question 3(b): How interpretations differ

Question 3(c): Why interpretations differ

Question 3(d): How far do you agree with one of the interpretations?

Revision techniques

Key topic 1 The Weimar Republic, 1918–29

The **Weimar Republic** faced challenges to its authority in its early years from 1919 to 1924. It experienced a period of recovery in the years 1924–29, during which there were important changes in society.

1 The origins of the Republic, 1918–19

The Weimar Republic was set up due to the legacy of the First World War.

1.1 The legacy of the First World War

Defeat in the First World War in 1918 led to revolution in Germany.

The Revolution of October/November 1918–19

- The First World War started in 1914 and the USA joined the Allies in the war against Germany in April 1917. By the early autumn of 1918, the German army was being pushed back in France. The British naval blockade had resulted in shortages of food for the German people. German defeat was imminent.

- In early October 1918, a new government was formed led by Prince Max of Baden. He approached US President Wilson about ending the war. Wilson said that he would not discuss peace terms with Germany while **Kaiser Wilhelm** and his military advisers were in control.

- At the end of October 1918, the German navy mutinied. Sailors at Kiel refused to put to sea and fight the British. Unrest began to spread across Germany.

- On 9 November, Kaiser Wilhelm's abdication was announced.

- On 10 November, a new republic was set up under Chancellor Ebert. The following day, Ebert signed the **armistice** with the Allies.

1.2 The setting up of the Weimar Republic

In January 1919, a new democratic **constitution** for Germany was drawn up. It was finalised in August 1919 and had both strengths and weaknesses.

Strengths of the new constitution

- It established the most advanced democracy in Europe – men and women had the vote at the age of 20 at a time when in Britain the age was 21 for men and 30 for women.

- The President was elected every seven years and had the power to appoint the Chancellor (head of the government).

- The Reichstag (parliament) had the power to pass or reject changes in the law. Members of the Reichstag were elected by **proportional representation** every four years.

- It established the right of free speech and freedom of religious belief.

Weaknesses of the new constitution

- Article 48 said that in an emergency the President could make laws without going to the Reichstag. This gave the President too much power.

- Proportional representation often led to many small parties gaining seats, including extremist groups such as the Nazis. No one party was large enough to secure a majority. **Coalition governments** were often weak and short lived.

- The army generals and judges were the same men who had served the Kaiser. Many of them opposed the Weimar Republic.

Key terms

Armistice The agreement to end hostilities in war

Coalition government Two or more political parties joining to form a government when no single political party gets a majority of the seats, in order to have sufficient support to pass laws

Constitution The basic principles according to which a country is governed

Proportional representation The number of votes won by a party determines the number of seats they get in parliament

Weimar Republic The republic that existed in Germany, 1919–33

Key individual

Kaiser Wilhelm The last German Emperor, ruling from 1888 to 1918

Revision task

Create a timeline showing the main developments in Germany, 1918–19, adding in dates and events.

Exam tip

You need to know the weaknesses of the German constitution, especially the effects of proportional representation and Article 48.

Strengths and weaknesses

1 Using the information on page 4, copy and complete both sides of the scales to show the strengths and weaknesses of the Weimar constitution.

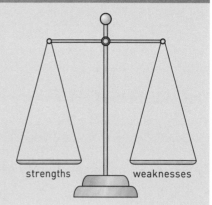

strengths   weaknesses

2 Do you think the strengths outweigh the weaknesses? Give reasons for your answer.

You're the examiner

1 Below are an exam-style question, a mark scheme and a paragraph written in answer to the question. Read the paragraph and the mark scheme and decide what mark you would give the answer.

Give two things you can infer from Source A about German reactions to the Versailles peace treaty. (4 marks)

SOURCE A

From a speech by Count Brockdorff-Rantzau, head of the German Versailles delegation to the Allied powers, 7 May 1919.

We shall be made to pay and, as the guilty, we shall be punished. We are required to admit that we alone are to blame for the war. Such an admission on my lips would be a lie. We emphatically deny that Germany, whose people were convinced that they were waging a war of defence, should be burdened with the sole responsibility for the war.

Mark scheme	
2 marks	1 mark for each valid inference up to a maximum of two inferences
2 marks	The second mark for each inference is for supporting detail selected from the source

STUDENT ANSWER

The source suggests that many Germans strongly opposed the War Guilt clause. The source also suggests that the War Guilt clause was unfair.

Mark [ ]   Reason _____

_____

2 Now write an answer which could gain 4 marks.

2 The early challenges to the Weimar Republic, 1919–23 [REVISED]

2.1 The early unpopularity of the Republic

The main reasons for the Republic's early unpopularity were the **'stab in the back' theory** and the **Treaty of Versailles**.

The 'stab in the back' theory

Many Germans thought the German army had been 'stabbed in the back' by the politicians ('the November Criminals') who signed the armistice in November 1918.

The key terms of the Treaty of Versailles

- The military terms reduced the German army to 100,000 and demilitarised the Rhineland. Germany was not allowed tanks, military aircraft or submarines.
- The territorial terms robbed Germany of key industrial areas, such as the iron of Alsace-Lorraine and the coalfields of the Saar. Germany lost thirteen per cent of its land.
- The financial terms seemed too harsh – with **reparations** set at £6.6 billion.
- Germany had to accept the blame for starting the war (the War Guilt clause).

Opponents of the Treaty described it as a *diktat* or dictated peace.

2.2 Challenges to the Republic from the left and right

The Republic faced threats from the left and right; there were several uprisings.

Opposition from the left – the Spartacists

- The **Spartacists**, led by Rosa Luxemburg and Karl Liebknecht, demonstrated against the government in December 1918. Sixteen people died in clashes with the army.
- They formed the German Communist Party and on 5 January 1919 staged an uprising in Berlin to overthrow the government and create a Communist state.
- The rising was crushed and Liebknecht and Luxemburg were killed.

Opposition from the right – the Kapp Putsch

- The *Freikorps* were furious about the Treaty of Versailles. In March 1920, they attempted to take power in Berlin, through a **putsch** led by Dr Wolfgang Kapp.
- Kapp set up a new right-wing government in Berlin. The army would not put the putsch down, showing its lack of support for the Weimar Republic.
- Berlin workers supported Weimar and went on strike; the putsch collapsed.

2.3 The challenges of 1923

The German government could not pay its first reparations payment. In January 1923, the French marched into the Ruhr industrial area, determined to get payment in kind by taking goods. The workers chose passive resistance to the occupation and went on strike. This meant that fewer goods were being produced. The German government printed more money to pay the strikers which, alongside fewer goods, turned inflation into **hyperinflation**. By November 1923, the German mark was worthless: $1 was worth 4,200,000,000 marks.

Hyperinflation losers	Hyperinflation winners
Old-age pensions became worthless	Businesses were able to pay off debts
People's savings lost all value	The rise in food prices helped farmers
Wages could not keep up with inflation and many people could not afford everyday necessities such as bread	

Key terms

Freikorps Private armies set up by German army officers at the end of the First World War; mainly consisted of ex-soldiers

Hyperinflation Extremely high inflation, where the value of the money plummets and it becomes almost worthless

Putsch An attempt to seize power by force

Reparations War damages (money) to be paid by Germany to countries it had fought against

Spartacists A Communist group who wanted to create a Communist state

'Stab in the back' theory The belief that Germany could have won the war and that politicians had stabbed the army in the back at the end of the war

Treaty of Versailles The peace treaty ending the First World War, signed on 28 June 1919

Revision task

Make a table to show the reasons for German discontent with the Treaty of Versailles, using these headings:

- military terms
- War Guilt
- Rhineland
- reparations
- loss of land.

Exam tip

Be aware of the terms of the Treaty of Versailles, how they affected Germany and why they brought widespread opposition.

RAG: Rate the timeline

Below are an exam-style question and a timeline. Read the question, study the timeline and, using three coloured pens, put a **red**, **amber** or **green** star next to the events to show:

Red: events and policies that have **no** relevance to the question

Amber: events and policies that have **some** relevance to the question

Green: events and policies that have **direct** relevance to the question.

Explain why there were challenges to the Weimar Republic in the years 1919–23.

> You may use the following in your answer:
> - The Spartacists
> - Hyperinflation
>
> You **must** also use information of your own.

1918 November Kaiser Wilhelm II abdicated

1918 November Germany signed the armistice

1918 November The 'stab in the back' theory

1920 Kapp Putsch

1924 Dawes Plan

1926 Germany joined League of Nations

1928 Kellogg–Briand Pact

| 1918 | 1919 | 1920 | 1921 | 1922 | 1923 | 1924 | 1925 | 1926 | 1927 | 1928 | 1929 |

1919 January Spartacist uprising

1919 June Signing of the Treaty of Versailles

1919 August Weimar constitution finalised

1923 French occupation of the Ruhr

1923 Hyperinflation

1923 Stresemann became foreign secretary

1925 Locarno Treaties

1929 Young Plan

Spot the mistakes

Below is a paragraph which is part of an answer to the question in the timeline activity above. However, it has factual mistakes. Identify the mistakes and on a separate piece of paper rewrite the paragraph.

> One reason why there were challenges to the Weimar Republic in the years 1919–23 was the presence of groups who wanted to form a Communist state. One of these groups was the Spartacist League, which was led by Karl Liebknecht and Gustav Stresemann. In December 1920, there were Spartacists' demonstrations against the government which led to clashes with the army and resulted in the deaths of sixteen Spartacists. At the end of the month, the Spartacists formed the Nazi Party. In January 1921, the Spartacists began their attempt to overthrow the Weimar government in order to create a Communist state. Ebert used the SS to put down the uprising.

3 The recovery of the Republic, 1924–29

The German economy recovered from the disasters of 1923 while relations with other countries, especially Britain and France, improved.

3.1 Reasons for economic recovery

There were several reasons for the economic recovery of the Republic, including:

- the role of Stresemann
- American loans
- the Rentenmark
- the Young Plan.
- the Dawes Plan

The role of Stresemann

In August 1923, **Gustav Stresemann** was appointed Chancellor to deal with the problems of hyperinflation. It was his decision to call off passive resistance in the Ruhr and to negotiate the **Dawes Plan**.

The Rentenmark

In November 1923, Stresemann introduced the **Rentenmark** to replace the German mark. This was a temporary measure in order to stabilise the currency and restore confidence. The Rentenmark's value was based on property values rather than on gold reserves. It was converted into the Reichsmark the following year, backed by gold reserves.

The Dawes Plan

The Dawes Plan of 1924 reorganised Germany's reparation payments:

- Payments were staged to match Germany's capacity to pay.
- Payments began at 1 billion marks for the first year and increased over a period of four years to 2.5 billion marks a year.
- In return, the French withdrew their troops from the Ruhr.

American loans

- The Dawes Plan also aimed to boost the German economy through US loans.
- Over the next six years, US companies and banks gave loans of nearly $3 billion.

The Young Plan

In 1929, Germany negotiated a further change to reparations known as the **Young Plan**:

- A timescale for payment was set, with Germany making payments until 1988.
- The reparation figure was reduced from £6 billion to £1.85 billion.

3.2 Stresemann's achievements abroad

Stresemann was responsible for several successes abroad that greatly assisted German recovery.

- Stresemann greatly improved relations with Britain and France by ending passive resistance in the Ruhr. The **Locarno Pact** of 1925 followed, signed by Germany, Britain, France, Italy and Belgium. By this agreement, Germany agreed to keep its existing borders.
- Germany had to become a member of the **League of Nations** for the Pact to come into operation. It was given a permanent seat in September 1926, which recognised its return to a Great Power.
- In 1928, Germany signed the **Kellogg–Briand Pact** along with 64 other nations. It was agreed that these nations would keep their armies for self-defence but would solve all future disputes by 'peaceful means'.

Key terms

Dawes Plan Introduced in 1924 to restructure Germany's annual reparations payments

Kellogg–Briand Pact International agreement to solve all disputes peacefully

League of Nations International body established after the First World War to maintain peace

Locarno Pact Series of agreements guaranteeing Germany's frontiers with neighbouring countries

Rentenmark New currency brought in by Stresemann to restore the value of the mark

Young Plan Introduced in 1929 to reduce German reparation payments

Key individual

Gustav Stresemann In 1919, he became leader of the German People's Party. From August to November 1923, he served as Chancellor of Germany and, later in the same year, he was appointed foreign secretary, a position he held until his death in 1929

Exam tips

1. Make sure you are aware of Stresemann's policies both at home and abroad.
2. You should have precise knowledge about the terms of both the Dawes Plan and the Young Plan. This will impress an examiner.

Quick quizzes at **www.hoddereducation.co.uk/myrevisionnotes**

Eliminate irrelevance

Below is an exam-style question:

Explain why the Weimar Republic recovered in the years 1924–29.

> You may use the following in your answer:
> - The Dawes Plan
> - The Locarno Pact
>
> You **must** also use information of your own.

Below is part of an answer to the question above. Some parts of the answer are not relevant to the question. Identify these and draw a line through the information that is irrelevant, justifying your deletions in the margin.

The Weimar government experienced hyperinflation in 1923. By November 1923 the German mark was worthless. Many people suffered due to the effects of hyperinflation, including pensioners who found that their pensions became worthless and people with savings who found that they lost all value.

German recovery in the years 1924–29 was partly due to the work of Stresemann who introduced the Dawes Plan which aimed to boost the German economy through US loans, beginning with a loan of 800 million marks. Reparations were sensibly staged to match Germany's capacity to pay. Reparation payments would begin at 1 billion marks for the first year and would increase over a period of four years to 2.5 billion a year. In return, France withdrew its troops from the Ruhr.

A further reason for German recovery was the Locarno Pact. Stresemann was determined to improve Germany's relations with Britain and France and restore German prestige abroad. The Locarno Pact of 1925, which also included Italy and Belgium, achieved all of these aims and guaranteed Germany's frontiers with France, Belgium and Italy. This, in turn, led to Germany being invited to join the League of Nations.

German recovery ended in 1929 with the Wall Street Crash in the USA. Many German businesses were forced to close. They were heavily dependent on loans from the USA.

German farmers also suffered as prices fell even more in the years after 1929.

 Choosing a third cause

To answer the exam-style question in the eliminate irrelevance activity above, you need to explain three causes. It is sensible to make use of the two given points. However, you will need to add one of your own. In the spaces below, write down your choice for a third point and the reasons behind it.

Reason: _____

_____

_____

Why I have chosen this reason: _____

_____

_____

Details to support this reason: _____

_____

_____

4 Changes in society, 1924–29

The period 1924–29 is often described as the 'golden age' of the Weimar Republic.

4.1 Changes in the standard of living

For many Germans, these years saw an improvement in their standard of living.

Wages

- The real value of wages increased each year after 1924 – benefiting German workers. By 1928, Germany had some of the best paid workers in Europe.
- While unemployment fell generally, it remained high in the professions such as lawyers, civil servants and teachers.

Housing

Weimar governments also attempted to deal with a shortage of housing. Between1924 and 1931 more than 2 million new homes were built and by 1928, homelessness had been reduced by more than 60 per cent.

Architecture

A new group of architects and designers emerged, called the *Bauhaus* who used bold designs and unusual materials, and basic shapes and colours.

Unemployment insurance

The Unemployment Insurance Law (1927) required workers and employees to make contributions to a national scheme for **unemployment welfare**.

4.2 Changes in the position of women

Debate about the status of women was an important feature of Weimar Germany.

Politics

- In 1919, women over 20 were given the vote.
- The Weimar constitution introduced equality in education, equal opportunity in civil service appointments and equal pay in the professions.
- By 1926, there were 32 women deputies in the Reichstag.

Leisure

Women enjoyed much more freedom, socially. They:

- went out unescorted and drank and smoked in public
- were fashion conscious, often wearing shorter skirts
- had their hair cut short and wore makeup.

Employment

- There was a growing number of women in new areas of employment, most noticeably in public employment such as the civil service and teaching, but also in shops and on the assembly line.
- Those women who worked in the civil service earned the same as men.
- By 1933, there were 100,000 women teachers and 3000 women doctors.

> **Key terms**
>
> *Bauhaus* An architectural and design movement – means 'School of Building'
>
> **Unemployment welfare** Payments made to the unemployed by the state

> **Revision task**
>
> Summarise in no more than ten words the changes to women in Germany in the years 1924–29.

> **Exam tip**
>
> Cultural changes are generally not as well revised as the recovery of the Republic under Stresemann. Ensure you have precise knowledge of these changes.

4.3 Cultural changes

Some of the most exciting art and culture in Europe emerged during this period.

Art

Neue Sachlichkeit (new objectivity) was a new approach to art which portrayed society in an objective way. It was associated with painters such as George Grosz and Otto Dix.

Cinema

This was a golden age for the German cinema. Fritz Lang was its best known director. He produced *Metropolis* (1927), the most technically advanced films of the decade. German actress Marlene Dietrich became one of the most popular films stars in the world, often playing strong and glamorous women.

 Inference

Below are an exam-style question and part of an answer.

Give two things you can infer from Source A about women in Weimar Germany.

Women had greater freedom socially. The details from the source which support this are the women who are shown in a bar drinking alcohol with men.

Now make a second inference and use details from the source to support it.

 Utility

Use the questions and statements in the white boxes around the photo to make notes in answer to the following question:

How useful is Source A for an enquiry into the position of women in the Weimar Republic in the 1920s? Explain your answer, using Source A and your knowledge of the historical context.

SOURCE A

A photograph showing women in a famous Berlin bar in the 1920s.

What is useful about the contents of the source?

What is useful about the nature, origins or purpose of the source?

Contextual knowledge to support your answer

In 1919–20, the **Nazi Party** was set up and, in the Munich Putsch of 1923, Hitler unsuccessfully tried to seize power by force. There was limited backing for the Nazis during 1924–28 but the Depression in 1929 brought increased support. Political developments in 1932 led to Hitler becoming Chancellor in 1933.

1 Early development of the Nazi Party, 1920–22
REVISED

The Nazi Party, led by Adolf Hitler, emerged in the early 1920s and was able to take advantage of the problems experienced by the Weimar Republic.

1.1 Hitler's early career

Hitler was born in Austria in 1889. When he was sixteen, he went to Vienna to become an artist. This did not work out. From 1908 to 1913 he was virtually a 'down-and-out' on the streets of Vienna. It was during these years that Hitler developed his hatred of Jews:

- **Anti-Semitism** was widespread in Vienna.
- He was envious of the wealthy Jews and blamed them for his own problems.

In 1914, Hitler joined the German army and served with distinction, winning the Iron Cross. He found it hard to accept the armistice, believing that Germany was on the verge of winning the war when it was betrayed by the politicians.

Hitler stayed in the army after the war, working for the intelligence services. He came across the **German Workers' Party (DAP)**, led by Anton Drexler, and joined it in 1919.

In 1920, the party was renamed the National Socialist German Workers' Party (NSDAP or Nazi Party).

1.2 The early growth and features of the Nazi Party

Hitler was good at public speaking and in February 1920 he was put in charge of recruitment and propaganda, attracting new members to the party. By 1921, he was strong enough to challenge Drexler and take over the leadership of the party himself.

- The political meetings generated much violence. In order to protect Nazi speakers, protection squads were used. These developed into the *Sturmabteilung* (**SA**) in 1921. It attracted many ex-soldiers, especially from the *Freikorps*. The SA would disrupt the meetings of Hitler's opponents, especially the Communists, and often beat up opposition supporters.
- By 1922, the Nazi Party had 6000 members, rising to 50,000 two years later.
- The Nazi Party drew up a **Twenty-Five Point Programme** (see box below). This was their political manifesto. It was vague and deliberately designed to appeal to as many groups as possible.

Key terms

Anti-Semitism Hatred of Jews

German Workers' Party (DAP) An anti-Weimar government party set up by Anton Drexler

Nationalise To change from private ownership to state ownership

Nazi Party The National Socialist German Workers' Party set up by Hitler in 1920

SA Hitler's private army set up to protect Nazi meetings and disrupt those of his opponents

Twenty-Five Point Programme The main aims and principles of the Nazi Party

Exam tip

You need to be aware of the impact of the DAP and the early Nazi Party on Hitler's career, including the Twenty-Five Point Programme and the setting up of the SA.

Key features of the Twenty-Five Point Programme

- The union of all Germans to form a Greater Germany.
- Getting rid of the Treaty of Versailles.
- Citizenship of the state to be granted only to people of German blood. Therefore no Jew was to be a citizen of the nation.
- The government to **nationalise** all businesses that had been formed into corporations.
- All newspaper editors and contributors to be German, and non-German papers to appear only with the permission of the government.

Inference

An inference is a message that you can get from a source by reading between the lines. Below are an exam-style inference question and a series of statements. Decide which of the statements:

- make(s) inferences from the source (I)
- paraphrase(s) the source (P)
- summarise(s) the source (S)
- cannot be justified from the source (X).

Give two things you can infer from Source A about Hitler's speeches.

SOURCE A

A member of the Nazi Party describing one of Hitler's speeches in 1922.

My critical faculty was swept away. Leaning forward as if he were trying to force his inner self into the consciousness of all these thousands, he was holding the masses, and me with them, under a hypnotic spell by the sheer force of his belief ... I forgot everything but the man; then glancing around, I saw that his magnetism was holding these thousands as one.

Statements	I	P	S	X
Hitler was holding the masses under a hypnotic spell				
Hitler attacked the Jews and the Weimar Republic in his speeches				
Hitler was a very effective speaker				
Hitler's speeches attracted many supporters to the Nazi Party				
Hitler's critical faculty was swept away and there were thousands of supporters				
Hitler made promises in his speeches				
He forgot everything but Hitler				
Hitler was able to impress people with the sheer force of his belief				

Identifying causation

Below is a list of statements about the early years of the Nazi Party. Identify with a tick which are statements of causation about the growth of the Nazi Party.

Hitler's qualities as a speaker brought increased membership of the Nazi Party	
The Twenty-Five Point Programme included destroying the Treaty of Versailles	
The establishment of the SA attracted more members to the Nazi Party	
The Twenty-Five Point Programme increased the appeal of the Nazi Party	
The DAP was renamed the Nazi Party	
The SA was used to protect Nazi meetings and attack the meetings of rival parties	

2 The Munich Putsch and the lean years, 1923–29

2.1 The Munich Putsch, 1923

In 1923, Hitler, supported by **General Ludendorff**, made his first attempt to seize power.

Background to the Putsch

● The Weimar Republic was more unpopular than ever due to the effects of hyperinflation.
● Hitler wanted to overthrow the Republic by organising a putsch in Bavaria and then march on Berlin.
● In 1922, the Italian leader, Mussolini, had successfully marched on Rome and taken over the Italian government with the support of the regular army. Hitler knew that he would have to win over the German army to be successful.
● Hitler thought the Bavarian leaders would support him, including Gustav von Kahr, Otto von Lossow and Hans Seisser.

Events of the Putsch

● On 8 November 1923, Hitler and the SA burst into a beer hall, disrupting a political meeting attended by Kahr, Seisser and Lossow.
● The three leaders were held at gunpoint until they offered their support for the Putsch. They were then released.
● The following day, Hitler and Ludendorff, with about 3000 supporters, including members of the SA, marched through Munich hoping to win mass public support. Seisser and Lossow had changed their minds and organised troops and police to resist them. Sixteen marchers were killed. Hitler fled.
● On 11 November, Hitler was arrested and the Nazi Party was banned.

Consequences of the Putsch

● In February 1924, Hitler was put on trial. The charge was high treason.
● Hitler turned his trial into a propaganda success, using it to attack the Weimar Republic. It provided him with nationwide publicity.
● The court was sympathetic to Hitler and gave him the minimum sentence for the offence – five years.
● Hitler was imprisoned in Landsberg Prison for only nine months. He wrote *Mein Kampf*, which contained his political views.
● Hitler realised that he needed complete control over the party and that in future he would try to gain power by legal methods – winning elections.

2.2 The lean years, 1924–29

The Nazi Party survived in secret until the ban was lifted in 1924. The period 1924–29 was a time of mixed fortunes for the Nazi Party.

Key individual

General Ludendorff
One of the German army leaders during the First World War. After the war, he criticised the new republic and accused it of having 'stabbed the army in the back'

Revision task

List the main changes to the Nazi Party in the years 1920–29. Put an arrow beside each to indicate whether it meant the party's fortunes were up, down or not altered by the change.

Exam tip

Remember to give a balanced evaluation of the Munich Putsch. Although it failed and Hitler was imprisoned, it did bring some benefits to Hitler and the Nazi Party.

The party did not do well	The party made progress
• There were quarrels and disagreements during Hitler's period in prison • Economic recovery meant there was little support for extremist parties • It only won twelve seats in the 1928 election	• It won 32 seats in the 1924 elections • *Mein Kampf* provided key ideas for the development of the Nazi Party with its focus on the importance of propaganda and anti-Semitism • Hitler reorganised the party to make it more efficient, with party branches run by *Gauleiters* • At the 1926 Bamberg party conference, Hitler continued to strengthen his position. Possible rivals to Hitler's leadership were won over or removed • Membership increased to 100,000 members by 1928

Below is an exam-style question.

Explain why the Nazi Party lost support in the years 1923–29.

You may use the following in your answer:
- The Munich Putsch
- Stresemann

You must also use information of your own.

1 Opposite is a mark scheme and below is a paragraph which is part of an answer to the question. Read the paragraph and the mark scheme. Decide which level you would award the paragraph. Write the level below, along with a justification for your choice.

Remember that for the higher levels, students must:

- explain at least three reasons
- focus explicitly on the question
- support their reasons with precise details.

Mark scheme

Level	Mark	
1	1–3	A simple or generalised answer is given, lacking development and organisation
2	4–6	An explanation is given, showing limited analysis and with implicit links to the question
3	7–9	An explanation is given, showing some analysis, which is mainly directed at the focus of the question
4	10–12	An analytical explanation is given which is directed consistently at the focus of the question

STUDENT ANSWER

On the second day of the Munich Putsch, Hitler and Ludendorff, with about 3000 supporters, some of whom were members of the SA, decided to march through Munich hoping to win mass public support. Armed police blocked their way and sixteen of the marchers were killed when the police opened fire. Hitler stayed in the background and then fled the battle. On 11 November Hitler was arrested for his part in the uprising.

Hitler was in prison for nine months.

Level ☐   Reason _____

_____

2 Now suggest what the student has to do to achieve a higher level.

_____

_____

_____

3 Try and rewrite this paragraph at a higher level.

4 Now try and write the rest of the answer to the question.

The Munich Putsch: Interpretation questions

Look at Sources A and B and Interpretations 1 and 2 below and then carry out the activities on page 17.

SOURCE A

A painting of the Munich Putsch of 1923 made later by one of its participants, showing the police opening fire on the Nazis. Hitler is standing with his arm raised and Erich von Ludendorff is on his right.

SOURCE B

From Hitler's recollections of the Munich Putsch, given in 1933.

It was the greatest good fortune for us Nazis that the Putsch collapsed because:

1   Co-operation with General Ludendorff would have been absolutely impossible.

2   The sudden takeover of power in the whole of Germany would have led to the greatest difficulties in 1923 because the essential preparations had not been made by the National Socialist Party.

3   The events of 9 November 1923, with their bloody sacrifice, have proven the most effective propaganda for National Socialism.

INTERPRETATION 1

From Germany 1858–1990: Hope, Terror and Revival *by A. Kitson, published in 2001.*

Kahr was forced to promise Hitler his support, but this support was short-lived. The next day it became clear to Hitler that neither Kahr nor the army were going to support his march. The Bavarian police were sent to stop the few thousand supporters that had gathered and opened fire, killing 16 Nazis. Hitler was driven away. Two days later he and other Nazi leaders were arrested and accused of high treason. The Nazi Party was banned and Hitler was Hitler was given the minimum sentence of five years' imprisonment.

INTERPRETATION 2

From Encyclopedia of the Third Reich *by Louis L. Snyder, published in 1998.*

On the surface the Beer-Hall Putsch seemed to be a failure, but actually it was a brilliant achievement for a political nobody. In a few hours Hitler catapulted his scarcely known, unimportant movement into headlines throughout Germany and the world. Moreover, he learned an important lesson: direct action was not the way to political power. It was necessary that he seek political victory by winning the masses to his side and also by attracting the support of wealthy industrialists. Then he could ease his way to political supremacy by legal means.

Quick quizzes at **www.hoddereducation.co.uk/myrevisionnotes**

Develop the detail

Below are an exam-style question and a paragraph which is part of an answer to the question. The paragraph contains a limited amount of detail. Annotate the paragraph to add additional detail to the answer.

Study Interpretations 1 and 2. They give different views on the consequences of the Munich Putsch of 1923. What is the main difference between the views? Explain your answer, using details from both interpretations.

> A main difference is that Interpretation 1 emphasises failures of the Munich Putsch. Interpretation 2 does not.

 Complete the paragraph

Below are an exam-style question and a paragraph which is part of an answer to this question. The paragraph gives a reason why the interpretations differ but does not give details from one of the sources to support this difference. Complete the paragraph adding the support from Sources A and B.

Suggest one reason Interpretations 1 and 2 give different views about the consequences of the Munich Putsch of 1923. You may use Sources A and B to help explain your answer.

> The interpretations may differ because they give different weight to different sources. For example, Source A provides some support for Interpretation 1, which stresses the defeat of Hitler's attempt to seize power and the failure of the Munich Putsch.

 Support or challenge?

Below is an exam-style question and below that are a series of general statements which are relevant to the question. Using your own knowledge and the information on page 42, write a C next to the statements that challenge the view given in Interpretation 2 about the Munich Putsch and write an S next to the statements that support the view in the interpretation.

How far do you agree with Interpretation 2 about the consequences of the 1923 Munich Putsch? Explain your answer, using both interpretations and your knowledge of the historical context.

Statement	Statement
Interpretation 2 suggests that the Munich Putsch was a brilliant success for Hitler	The Nazi Party was weak after the Putsch because Hitler was in prison and there were arguments and differences between the leading members
Hitler was a laughing stock because he had fled the gunfight in the street	Interpretation 1 suggests that the aftermath of the Putsch was a failure, with the Nazi Party banned and Hitler arrested
Interpretation 1 stresses the failures of the Munich Putsch, especially when the Nazis were stopped by the Bavarian police	The court was sympathetic to Hitler. Instead of sentencing him to death as it might have done, it gave him the minimum sentence for the offence – five years
Hitler turned his trial into a propaganda success, using it to attack the Weimar Republic whom he accused of treason because of the armistice and signing the Treaty of Versailles	Hitler and the Nazis had failed to get the support of the leaders of Bavaria
Interpretation 2 suggests that the Munich Putsch encouraged Hitler to change his tactics for achieving power	Hitler spent most of his time in prison writing *Mein Kampf* (*My Struggle*)

3 The growth in support for the Nazis, 1929–32

3.1 The growth of unemployment – causes and impact

In October 1929, the **Wall Street Crash** led to US loans being recalled and, as a result, many German businesses sacked workers and were forced to close. German farmers also suffered as prices fell further. By 1932, over 6 million people were unemployed. The Weimar Republic failed to deal with unemployment and lost support. There was a growth in support for right- and left-wing parties, such as the Nazi Party and Communist Party.

- The Weimar Republic was blamed for allowing the economy to become too dependent on US loans.
- There was disagreement in government about the level of unemployment contributions. Chancellor Müller resigned in March 1930.
- Brüning became Chancellor after Müller. Brüning's reduction of government spending, pay cuts, cuts to unemployment benefit and increase in taxes lost him support. In May 1932, he resigned.
- Elections were called in July and November 1932. The Communist Party gained 100 seats (16.9%) in the November 1932 elections.

> **Key term**
>
> **Wall Street Crash**
> Collapse of the US stock market on 29 October 1929 leading to the Depression and world economic crisis

3.2 Reasons for growth in support for the Nazi Party

In the September 1930 elections, the Nazi Party won 107 seats and, by July 1932, it was the largest party, with 230 seats. This increased support was due to several reasons. Three of the main ones are outlined below.

Hitler

- Posters and rallies built Hitler up as a superman. The campaigns focused around his personality and his skills, especially as a speaker.
- Unemployment had hit everyone; thus Hitler tried to appeal to all sections of society. The Nazi message was that the Weimar Republic had caused the economic crisis and that weak coalition governments had no real solutions to offer. The Nazis alone could unite Germany in a time of economic crisis.
- Hitler provided the German people with a scapegoat – blaming the Jews for Germany's problems.
- Hitler won support from business and industrialists who donated funds to the Nazi Party. They were especially concerned at increased support for the Communist Party.

The SA

- By 1932, the SA numbered 600,000. It organised parades through towns and cities, impressing many Germans who saw order and discipline in a time of chaos.
- It was used to intimidate any opposition, especially the Communists.

Goebbels

Josef Goebbels was a master of propaganda and used every possible method to get across the Nazi message:

- Posters targeted different audiences and were timed to have maximum impact. Their message was generally simple but clear.
- He chartered planes to fly Hitler all over Germany to speak at four or five rallies per day.

> **Key individual**
>
> **Josef Goebbels** Joined the Nazi Party in 1922 and, in 1928, was elected to the Reichstag. Appointed head of propaganda of the Nazi Party in 1929. In 1933 he was appointed Minister of Public Propaganda and Enlightenment

> **Revision task**
>
> Using pages 12–18, produce a list of factors that changed the fortunes of the Nazis between the beginning of the 1920s and the early 1930s.

> **Exam tip**
>
> Remember that Germany was affected by hyperinflation in 1923, not during the Depression of 1929–32.

Concentric circles

In the concentric circles, rank order the following reasons for increased support for the Nazis in the years 1929–32, beginning with the most important in the middle to the least important on the outside. Explain your decisions.

- the Depression
- Hitler's appeal
- Nazi propaganda
- the SA.

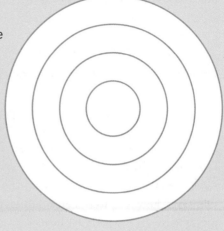

 Focusing on the question

Below is an exam-style question.

Explain why there was increased support for the Nazis in the years 1929–32.

> You may use the following in your answer:
> - **The Depression**   ■ **Hitler**
>
> You **must** also use information of your own.

It is important that you make it clear in your answer that you are focusing on the question. Look at the paragraph below, which is part of an answer to the question.

The wording of the question is used.

One important reason for increased Nazi support in the years 1929–32 was the Depression. This was because the Depression brought about great hardship for many German people and increased the level of unemployment to over 6 million by 1932. The Nazi Party was able to appeal to a significant number of these unemployed people.

The information about the Depression focuses on increased support for the Nazis.

Now write another paragraph in answer to the question.

4 How Hitler became Chancellor, 1932–33

Political instability and the eventual, reluctant, support of President **Hindenburg** brought Hitler to power as Chancellor in January 1933.

4.1 Political developments in 1932

A series of changes of government in 1932 further weakened the Weimar Republic:

- After Brüning stepped down in May 1932, **Franz von Papen**, a friend of President Hindenburg, was appointed Chancellor. He was leader of the Centre Party but only had 68 supporters in the Reichstag and was dependent on government by decree.
- In July 1932, von Papen held elections, hoping to gain more support. The elections, however, were a great success for the Nazis, who won 230 seats and became the largest party in the Reichstag. Hitler demanded the post of Chancellor. Hindenburg, who disliked Hitler, refused to appoint him.
- In November, von Papen arranged another election for the Reichstag, hoping to win more support. This time he won even fewer seats. The Nazi Party's seats fell to 196.
- Von Papen suggested abolishing the Weimar constitution. Von Schleicher, an army leader, persuaded Hindenburg that this would result in civil war. Hindenburg lost confidence in von Papen, who resigned.
- In the following month, Hindenburg appointed von Schleicher as Chancellor, who lasted less than two months.

4.2 The part played by Hindenburg and von Papen

- Von Papen was determined to regain power. To this end he met Hitler in early January 1933 when they agreed that Hitler should lead a government with von Papen as the Vice-Chancellor.
- They had the support of the army, major landowners and leaders of industry who disliked von Schleicher's plans to bring together different strands from the left and right parties and were worried about a Communist takeover.
- Von Papen convinced President Hindenburg that a coalition government with Hitler as Chancellor would save Germany and bring stability. Von Papen said that he would be able to control Hitler – he would 'make Hitler squeak'.
- On 31 January 1933, Hindenburg invited Hitler to become Chancellor.

Key individuals

Paul von Hindenburg
A leading general in the First World War, becoming chief of the general staff in 1916. He retired from the army in 1918 and supported the 'stab in the back' theory. President of Germany 1925–34

Franz von Papen Entered politics in 1918 as a member of the Catholic Centre Party and four years later was elected to the Reichstag. He eventually became a favourite of Hindenburg. When Hitler became Chancellor, in January 1933, von Papen was his Vice-Chancellor

Revision task

Summarise the part played by the following in Hitler's rise to power:

- Hindenburg
- von Schleicher
- von Papen.

Exam tip

The events of 1932 are very complex. However, you will need a thorough knowledge of what took place, especially the role of Hindenburg and von Papen.

Understand the chronology

Place the events between March 1932 and January 1933 listed below in the correct chronological sequence in the timeline.

Date	Event
March 1932	
April	
May	
June	
July	
August	
September	
October	
November	
December	
January 1933	

EVENTS

A Hitler demanded the post of Chancellor. Hindenburg refused to appoint him

B Von Papen arranged for another election for the Reichstag, hoping to win more support

C Hindenburg appointed von Schleicher, an army leader, as Chancellor

D Von Papen became Chancellor

E The Nazis' seats fell to 196

F The Nazis won 230 seats, becoming the largest party in the Reichstag

G Hitler became Chancellor of Germany

H Chancellor Brüning was forced to resign

I Hindenburg invited Hitler to become Chancellor

J Von Papen and Hitler agreed that Hitler should become Chancellor and von Papen Vice-Chancellor

 ## Utility

Below are a utility question and an answer focusing on the utility of the contents of the source. On a separate piece of paper complete the answer by explaining the utility of the nature, origins and purpose of the source. You could look at page 42 for guidance on how to answer the utility question to help you.

How useful is Source A for an enquiry into the political developments in Germany, 1932–33, which led to Hitler being appointed Chancellor? Explain your answer, using Source A and your knowledge of the historical context.

SOURCE A

A cartoon from the British magazine Punch, *January 1933.*

'The Temporary Triangle. Von Hindenburg and Von Papen (together): "For He's a Jolly Good Fellow, For He's a Jolly Good Fellow, For He's a Jolly Good Fellow," (aside: "Confound him!") "And So Say Both of Us".'

Source A is useful because it suggests that Hitler became Chancellor because of the actions of Hindenburg and von Papen. This is shown in the cartoon with Hitler being carried by the two men who are singing 'for he's a jolly good fellow'. This is supported by my knowledge of the events which brought Hitler to power. Von Papen and Hindenburg did work together to make Hitler Chancellor. Von Papen met Hitler in early January 1933 where they agreed that Hitler should lead a government with von Papen as the Vice-Chancellor. Von Papen then convinced President Hindenburg that a coalition government with Hitler as Chancellor would save Germany and bring stability. Von Papen said that he would be able to control Hitler – he would 'make Hitler squeak'.

Key topic 3 Nazi control and dictatorship, 1933–39

From January 1933 to August 1934, the Nazis secured control of all aspects of the German state. Hitler then consolidated his dictatorship through setting up a police state and using propaganda and censorship.

1 The creation of a dictatorship, 1933–34

1.1 Setting up the dictatorship

From January 1933 to August 1934, Hitler secured control of the German state, removing all opposition.

The Reichstag Fire, February 1933

- On 27 February 1933, the **Reichstag** building was burned down. A Dutch Communist, Marius van der Lubbe, was put on trial and found guilty of starting the fire. Hitler blamed the Communist Party for the fire.
- Hitler persuaded Hindenburg to pass an emergency decree – the 'Decree for the Protection of the People and the State' – giving the police powers to detain people without trial.

The Enabling Act, March 1933

The 'Enabling Act' gave Hitler the power to make laws without the Reichstag's consent. Using these powers, Hitler:

- Removed further opposition to the Nazi government, including banning all **trade unions**. The unions were merged into a 'German Labour Front'.
- Banned all other political parties. By July 1933, Germany was a one-party state.

1.2 The Night of the Long Knives, 30 June 1934

The SA (see page 18) led by Röhm was a threat to Hitler's power. He removed this threat by purging the SA in the **Night of the Long Knives**.

Reasons for the purge

- The SA were increasingly out of control at a time when Hitler was trying to establish a dictatorship through legal methods.
- Röhm wanted a social revolution: to bring about greater equality in society.
- Leading Nazis such as Himmler were concerned about Röhm's growing influence. Himmler wanted to replace the SA with his own **SS**.

Events of the Night of the Long Knives

- Hitler arranged a meeting with Röhm and 100 other SA leaders. They were arrested by the SS, taken to Munich and shot.
- About 400 people were murdered in the purge.

Results

- Hitler got rid of would-be opponents.
- The SA now had a minor role.
- After Hindenburg died in August 1934, the army leaders swore an **oath of allegiance** to Hitler, giving him unconditional obedience.

1.3 Hitler becomes Führer

After Hindenburg's death, Hitler declared himself '**Führer**', combining the post of Chancellor and President. He called a referendum and more than 90 per cent of the voters (38 million) agreed with his action.

Key terms

Führer German title meaning leader

Night of the Long Knives 30 June 1934, when Hitler purged Röhm and the SA

Oath of allegiance A promise made by the German armed forces to be loyal to Hitler

Reichstag German state parliament

SS *Schultzstaffel* or 'protection squad'. Originally Hitler's bodyguards, they became the most powerful troops in the Third Reich, and wore distinctive black uniforms

Trade unions Organisations set up to protect and improve the rights of workers

---

Revision task

Draw a timeline for the creation of a dictatorship from January 1933 to August 1934. On the timeline include the key events which helped Hitler to create a Nazi dictatorship.

Exam tip

Ensure you thoroughly revise the sequence of events in 1933, beginning with when Hitler became Chancellor until the death of Hindenburg.

Identify the view

 hidden

Identify the view

Read the interpretation and identify the view that is offered about the Reichstag fire of February 1933.

INTERPRETATION 1

From Germany 1866–1945 by S. Eddy and T. Lancaster, published in 2002.

The popular view, especially among foreign journalists, was that since the Nazis had most to gain that they set fire to the Reichstag. It has been argued, for example, that the fire was too big to have been the work of one man, van der Lubbe, and that the timing of the fire, six days before the election, was simply too convenient for the Nazis.

1 What view is offered by the interpretation about the Reichstag fire?

_____

_____

2 a) Now use your knowledge to agree with or contradict the view given in the interpretation. To plan an answer to this question, make a copy of and complete the following table.

View given in interpretation	
Knowledge which supports this view	
Knowledge which contradicts this view	

   b) Write a paragraph supporting and challenging this view.

RAG: Rate the timeline

Below are an exam-style question and a timeline. Read the question, study the timeline and, using three coloured pens, put a **red**, **amber** or **green** star next to the events to show:

Red: events and policies that have **no** relevance to the question

Amber: events and policies that have **some** relevance to the question

Green: events and policies that have **direct** relevance to the question.

> You may use the following in your answer:
> - **The Reichstag fire (1933)**
> - **The Night of the Long Knives (1934)**
>
> You **must** also use information of your own.

Explain why Hitler was able to establish a dictatorship of the Nazi Party in the years 1933–34.

1934 June The Night of the Long Knives

1932 May Von Papen became Chancellor

1932 July The Nazis became the largest party in the Reichstag

1932 November Von Schleicher became Chancellor

1934 August Hindenburg died

1934 August Hitler combined the posts of Chancellor and Führer

1934 Local councils banned Jews from public places

1932	1933	1934	1935

1933 January Hitler appointed Chancellor

1933 February The Reichstag fire

1933 March The Enabling Act

1933 April The boycott of Jewish shops

1933 May Trade unions banned

1933 July The Nazis became the only legal party in Germany

1935 The Nuremberg Laws were passed, denying the Jews citizenship of Germany

2 The police state

2.1 The Gestapo, SS, SD and concentration camps

The Nazis created a police state through the use of these different agencies – establishing a climate of fear.

The SS (protection squad)

- Led by Himmler, the SS were responsible for the removal of all opposition and became the main means of intimidating Germans into obedience.
- By 1934, the SS had more than 50,000 members, growing to 250,000 by 1939.

The Gestapo (secret police)

- Set up in 1933 by Goering, in 1936 the **Gestapo** came under the control of Himmler and the SS.
- It could arrest and imprison without trial those suspected of opposing the state.
- Only it had the power to send political opponents to **concentration camps**.

The SD

- Set up in 1931, the **SD** was the intelligence agency of the Nazi Party under the command of Himmler, and organised by Heydrich.
- Its main aim was to find actual and potential enemies of the Nazi Party and ensure that they were removed.

Concentration camps

- In 1933, the Nazis established concentration camps to detain political prisoners. These were run by the SS and SD.
- Prisoners were classified into different categories, each denoted by wearing a different coloured triangle. For example, black triangles were for vagrants and red triangles were for political prisoners.
- By 1939, there were more than 150,000 people under arrest for political offences.

2.2 Nazi control of the legal system

Hitler wanted to ensure that all laws were interpreted in a Nazi fashion:

- All judges had to become members of the National Socialist League for the Maintenance of Law. This meant Nazi views were upheld in the courts.
- In 1934, the People's Court was established to try cases of treason. The judges were loyal Nazis.
- In October 1933, the German Lawyers Front was established. Lawyers had to swear that they would 'follow the course of the Führer'. There were more than 10,000 members by the end of the year.

2.3 Nazi policies towards the Churches

In Germany, about two-thirds of the people were Protestant and one-third was Roman Catholic.

The Catholic Church

Hitler was determined to reduce the influence of the Catholic Church:

- Catholics owed their first allegiance to the Pope, not Hitler. They had divided loyalties. Hitler said a person was either a Christian or a German but not both.
- There were Catholic schools and youth organisations whose message to the young was at odds with that of the Nazi Party.

In 1933, Hitler signed a **Concordat** agreeing not to interfere with the Catholic Church. In return, the Catholic Church agreed to stay out of politics. Within a year, Hitler began to break the agreement and attack the Catholic Church:

- Catholic schools were made to remove Christian symbols and were eventually abolished.
- Priests were harassed and arrested. Many criticised the Nazis and ended up in concentration camps.
- Catholic youth movements were closed down.

The Protestant Church

In 1933, Protestant groups which supported the Nazis united to form the '**Reich Church**'. Its leader, Ludwig Müller, became the first Reich Bishop in September 1933.

Many Protestants opposed Nazism, which they believed conflicted with their Christian beliefs. They were led by Pastor Niemöller (see page 28). In December 1933, they set up the Pastors' Emergency League for those who opposed Hitler.

(see page 28)

Inference

An inference is a message that you can get from a source by reading between the lines. Below are an exam-style inference question, the source and a series of statements. Decide which of the statements:

- make(s) inferences from the source (I)
- summarise(s) the source (S)
- cannot be justified from the source (X).

Give two things you can infer from Source A about the Nazi police state.

SOURCE A

An incident reported in the Rhineland, July 1938.

In a café, a 64-year-old woman remarked to her companion at the table: 'Mussolini [the leader of Italy] has more political sense in one of his boots than Hitler has in his brain.' The remark was overheard and five minutes later the woman was arrested by the Gestapo who had been alerted by telephone.

Statements	I	S	X
People were frightened of the Gestapo			
A woman suggested that Mussolini had more sense than Hitler			
The Nazis made use of informers and spies			
Many people were arrested by the Gestapo			
You were not allowed to criticise Hitler and the Nazis			
A woman was arrested because she criticised Hitler			

Spot the mistakes

Below is a paragraph about the Churches in the police state. However, it has factual mistakes. Identify the mistakes and rewrite the paragraph.

In Germany, most of the population was Roman Catholic. At first Hitler decided to cooperate with the Catholic Church. In 1935, he signed an agreement known as a Concordat. In 1933, those Protestant groups that supported the Nazis agreed to unite to form the 'Reich Church'. Their leader, Pastor Niemöller, became the first Reich Bishop in September 1933. Many Protestants opposed Nazism, which they believed conflicted greatly with their own Christian beliefs. They were led by Ludwig Müller and, in December 1934, they set up the Reich League for those who opposed Hitler.

3 Controlling and influencing attitudes

REVISED

3.1 Goebbels and the Ministry of Propaganda

Censorship and propaganda were used to ensure that people accepted and conformed to Nazi thinking. In 1933, Goebbels was appointed as Minister of Public Propaganda and Enlightenment.

Censorship

- No book could be published without Goebbels' permission.
- Newspapers that opposed Nazi views were closed down. Editors were told what could be printed.
- The radio was controlled.

Propaganda

- Posters were used to put across the Nazi message.
- Goebbels ordered the mass production of cheap radios. By 1939, 70 per cent of German homes had a radio. It was important that the Nazi message was heard.
- Mass rallies and marches projected the image of power and terror. Every year a party rally was held at Nuremberg.
- Success in sport was important to promote the Nazi regime.

The Berlin Olympics of 1936

- A major sporting showcase, the Olympics was designed to impress the outside world and was a public relations success.
- Hitler's plans to highlight the superiority of the **Aryan** race were sabotaged by the success of the black athletes in the US Olympic team, especially Jesse Owens, who won the 100 metres, 200 metres, long jump and 4 × 100 metres relay.

3.2 Nazi control of culture and the arts

The Nazis used culture and arts to promote their ideals. Artists were encouraged to use 'Aryan themes' such as the family, national community and heroism.

Music

Hitler hated modern music. Jazz, which was 'black' music, was seen as racially inferior and was banned. Instead, the Nazis promoted traditional German folk music and the classical music of Brahms, Beethoven and especially Richard Wagner.

Films

The Nazis also controlled the cinema. All films were accompanied by a 45-minute official newsreel which glorified Hitler and Germany.

Art

Hitler hated modern art, which he believed was backward, unpatriotic and Jewish. Such art was called 'degenerate', and banned. Art highlighting Germany's past greatness and the strength and power of the **Third Reich** was encouraged.

Theatre

Theatre concentrated on German history and political drama. Cheap theatre tickets were available to encourage people to see plays which often had a Nazi political or racial theme.

Key terms

Aryan Nazi term for someone of supposedly 'pure' German stock

Censorship Controlling what is produced and suppressing anything considered against the state

Third Reich Nazi name for Germany. Means 'Third Empire'

Revision task

How were the following used by the Nazis to maintain their dictatorship?

- the radio
- cinema
- sport.

Exam tips

1 Do not confuse Goebbels' propaganda methods before and after Hitler came to power.
2 Remember that Nazi control was based on fear, through the police state, and persuasion, through censorship and propaganda.

Architecture

Hitler encouraged the 'monumental style' for public buildings. These large stone buildings were often copies from ancient Greece or Rome and showed the power of the Third Reich. Hitler admired the Greek and Roman style of building because he said the Jews had not 'contaminated' it.

Literature

All books, plays and poems were carefully censored and controlled to put across the Nazi message. Encouraged by Goebbels, students in Berlin burned 20,000 books written by Jews, Communists and anti-Nazi university professors in a massive bonfire in Berlin in May 1933.

 How important

Complete the table below.
- Briefly summarise why each factor enabled Hitler to establish his dictatorship in the years 1933–39.
- Make a decision about the importance of each factor in achieving and maintaining Hitler's dictatorship. Give a brief explanation for each choice.

Factor	Key features	Decisive/important/quite important
Reichstag fire		
The Enabling Act		
The SA		
The Night of the Long Knives		
Law courts		
SS and Gestapo		
Concentration camps		
Churches		
Censorship		
Propaganda		

Causation

Below is an exam-style question.

Explain why the Nazi Party was able to establish a dictatorship in Germany in the years 1933–39.

> You may use the following in your answer:
> - The SS
> - Censorship
>
> You **must** also use information of your own.

To answer the question above, you need to explain three causes. It is sensible to make use of the two given points. However, you will need to explain a third cause. You could select one of these from the table in the 'How important' activity above. Write down your choice and the reasons behind it.

Cause: _____

_____

Why I have chosen this cause: _____

_____

Details to support this cause: _____

_____

4 Opposition, resistance and conformity

REVISED

Between 1933 and 1939, about 1.3 million people were sent to concentration camps, seeming to indicate quite widespread opposition to the regime. It has also been estimated that about 300,000 people left Germany. However, although there was some opposition it was never co-ordinated or enough to threaten the regime in the years 1933–39.

4.1 The extent of support for the Nazi regime

Many Germans gained much from Hitler's successes after 1933 and consequently supported him:

- There were economic successes which began to erase the Depression (see page 18).
- Germany's international standing grew, seeming to remove the shame of the Treaty of Versailles. The Saar was returned in 1935, the army was built up after 1935 and in 1936 the Rhineland was remilitarised.
- Some Germans were happy to see the Communists, Socialists and SA leaders removed.

4.2 Opposition from the Churches

- Many Catholic priests opposed Nazi policies and were arrested. At least 400 were sent to Dachau concentration camp. In many respects this had the opposite effect to what the Nazis wanted. Priests who were sent to concentration camps were seen as **martyrs**. Catholic Churches were packed every Sunday.
- Many Protestant pastors opposed Hitler and the Reich Church. They were led by Pastor Niemöller, who set up the '**Confessional Church**'. **Niemöller** and many other pastors were arrested and sent to concentration camps. Nazi repression did not destroy Protestant opposition. Instead it created martyrs.

4.3 Opposition from the young

Although many young people joined the **Hitler Youth**, it was not popular with some of its members. Not all young people accepted the Nazi ideas and some set up other groups.

The Edelweiss Pirates

The **Edelweiss Pirates** were not a unified group but a loose band across many cities, first emerging in 1934. In Cologne they were called the Navajos, and Essen had the Roving Dudes.

- They listened to forbidden swing music and daubed walls with anti-Nazi graffiti.
- They could be recognised by their badges, for example the *edelweiss* or skull and crossbones.
- They wore clothes which were considered outlandish by the Nazis – checked shirts, dark short trousers and white socks.
- By 1939 they had a membership of 2000.
- They created no-go areas for Hitler Youth in their cities.

The Swing Youth

Swing Youth tended to come from the middle classes. They loved swing music, which was hated by the Nazis who classed it as non-German, developed by 'Negros' and Jews. They rebelled against the order and discipline of the Nazis and took part in activities which were frowned upon.

Key terms

Confessional Church Protestant Church set up by Pastor Niemöller in opposition to the Reich Church

Edelweiss Pirates A loosely organised youth group who rebelled against Nazi ideas

Hitler Youth Organisation set up for the young to convert them to Nazi ideals

Martyr A person who is persecuted and/or killed because of their religious or other beliefs

Swing Youth Young people who loved swing music and challenged Nazi views about the young

---

Key individual

Martin Niemöller Served in the German navy as a U-boat commander during the First World War. In 1929 became a pastor in the Protestant Church and a supporter of Hitler. Began to criticise Hitler when, from 1937, members of the Protestant Church were arrested. Survived seven years in a concentration camp before being released in 1945

Revision task

Give two reasons why there was little opposition to the Nazi regime.

Eliminate irrelevance

Below is an exam-style question and part of an answer. Some parts of the answer are not relevant to the question. Identify these and draw a line through the information that is irrelevant, justifying your deletions in the margin.

Explain why there was opposition to the Nazi regime in the years 1933–39.

> You may use the following in your answer:
> - The Catholic Church
> - The Edelweiss Pirates
>
> You **must** also use information of your own.

One reason for opposition to the Nazi policies was the Catholic Church. Hitler decided to cooperate with the Catholic Church. In 1933, Hitler signed an agreement known as a Concordat. Hitler promised not to interfere with the Catholic Church. In return, the Catholic Church agreed to stay out of politics. Many Catholic priests criticised Nazi policies and were arrested and sent to Dachau concentration camp. In many respects this had the opposite effect to what the Nazis wanted. Priests who were sent to concentration camps were seen as martyrs and encouraged even more opposition to the Nazis.

There was also opposition to the Nazi regime from young people. The Nazis set up the Hitler Youth. There were four separate organisations that were developed which recruited girls and boys from the ages of 10–18 under the control of Baldur von Shirach, Youth Leader of the Reich. One group that opposed the Nazis was the Edelweiss Pirates. Its members rebelled against Nazi ideas by listening to forbidden swing music and daubed walls with anti-Nazi graffiti. They could be recognised by their badges, for example the *edelweiss* or skull and crossbones. They wore clothes which were considered outlandish by the Nazis – check shirts, dark short trousers and white socks.

 Memory map

Use the information on page 28 to add details to the diagram below about opposition, resistance and conformity.

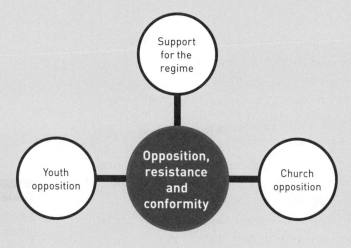

This topic examines how the lives of German citizens were changed by Nazi policies. It considers the Nazis' racial policies and their persecution of Jews and other minority groups.

1 Nazi policies towards women

REVISED

The Nazis had a traditional view of the role of women. Their policies reflected this.

1.1 Nazi views on women and the family

The Nazis wanted to reverse the developments of the 1920s (see page 10). They thought women should be homemakers and childbearers, and not go out to work. Their slogan '*Kinder, Kirche, Küche*' summed up their view:

- They wanted to increase the birth rate and strengthen the Third Reich.
- Women had a central role in producing the genetically pure Aryan race, ensuring the future of a strong Nazi state.

1.2 Nazi policies towards women

Nazi policies brought about changes in women's employment, domestic roles and appearance.

- *Employment*: women were encouraged to give up their jobs, get married and have large families. Women doctors, civil servants and teachers were forced to leave their professions. Girls were discouraged from higher education and gaining the qualifications needed for professional careers.

- *Marriage and family*: in 1933, the Law for the Encouragement of Marriage provided loans to help young couples marry, as long as the wife left her job. Couples kept one-quarter of the loan for each child born, up to four children. Maternity benefits were also increased. On Hitler's mother's birthday (12 August) medals were awarded to women with large families.

- *Appearance*: the ideal Nazi woman was blonde, blue-eyed and sturdily built with broad hips for childbearing. She wore traditional clothes and did not smoke or drink. Women were discouraged from wearing trousers, high heels and makeup. Dyeing or styling hair was frowned on, as was slimming, which was seen as bad for childbearing.

1.3 Successes and failures of Nazi policies

There were successes:

- In the first few years the number of married women in employment fell.
- The number of marriages and the birth rate increased.
- The German Women's Enterprise organised Mothers' Schools to train women in household skills, as well as courses, lectures and radio programmes on household topics. It had 6 million members.

However, there were limitations and even failures:

- The number of women in employment increased from 4.85 million in 1933 to 7.14 million in 1939. From 1936 there was a labour shortage and more workers were needed in heavy industry due to rearmament.
- Many employers preferred women workers because they were cheaper. Women's wages remained only two-thirds of men's.
- Some women resented the loss of more professional jobs such as doctors, lawyers and schoolteachers.

> **Key term**
>
> *Kinder, Kirche, Küche*
> Nazi slogan meaning Children, Church and Cooking

> **Revision task**
>
> How do you explain the following? The Nazis believed that a woman's place was in the home and yet more women were in employment by 1939.

> **Exam tip**
>
> Remember that women had an important family and childbearing role in Nazi Germany.

You're the examiner

Below is an exam-style question.

Explain why the position of women changed in Nazi Germany in the years 1933–39.

1 Below are a mark scheme and a paragraph which is part of an answer to the question. Read the paragraph and the mark scheme. Decide which level you would award the paragraph. Write the level below, along with a justification for your choice.

> You may use the following in your answer:
> ■ Employment   ■ Appearance
> You **must** also use information of your own.

Mark scheme

Level	Mark	
1	1–3	A simple or generalised answer is given, lacking development and organisation
2	4–6	An explanation is given, showing limited analysis and with only an implicit link to the question
3	7–9	An explanation is given, showing some analysis, which is mainly directed at the focus of the question
4	10–12	An analytical explanation is given which is directed consistently at the focus of the question

Remember that for the higher levels, students must

● explain at least three reasons

● focus explicitly on the question

● support their reasons with precise details.

STUDENT ANSWER

The ideal Nazi woman was blonde, blue-eyed and sturdily built. She was expected to have broad hips for childbearing and to wear traditional, not fashionable clothes. She did not wear makeup nor did she smoke or drink. Losing weight was frowned on because it could be bad for childbearing.

The Nazis believed that a woman's place was in the home and were determined to get women to give up their jobs. Instead, they wanted them to get married and have large families. Women in the professions such as doctors and civil servants had to give up their jobs. Labour exchanges and employers were encouraged to give first choice of jobs to men. Women had a much more domestic role.

Level ☐   Reason _____

_____

2 Now suggest what the student has to do to achieve a higher level.

_____

_____

3 Try and rewrite this paragraph at a higher level.

4 Now try and write the rest of the answer to the question.

2 Nazi policies towards the young

The Nazis tried to make young people into loyal Nazis through controlling education and youth movements.

2.1 Nazi control of the young through education

Teachers had to accept and put across Nazi ideals or be sacked. Nearly all joined the Nazi Teachers' Association.

The curriculum changed to put across key Nazi ideals and prepare students for their future roles. Textbooks were rewritten to fit the Nazi view of history and racial purity and had to be approved by the Ministry of Education. *Mein Kampf* became a standard text.

With boys, the emphasis was on preparation for the military. Girls learned needlework and cookery to become good homemakers and mothers.

- History: this was rewritten to glorify Germany's past and the Nazi Party.
- Physical education: took fifteen per cent of curriculum time to ensure that girls were fit to be mothers and boys were prepared for military service.
- Eugenics: a new subject about selective breeding, more especially the creation of a master race. Children were taught that they should not marry so-called inferior races, such as Jews.
- Race studies: a new subject to put forward Nazi ideas on race, in particular the superiority of the Aryan race.
- Geography: pupils were taught about lands which were once part of Germany and the need for more living space (*lebensraum*) for Germans.

2.2 Hitler Youth and the League of German Maidens

The Nazis wanted to control the leisure time of the young. They closed down all youth movements belonging to other political parties and the Churches. There were four separate youth organisations for 10–18-year-olds, under the control of Baldur von Shirach, Youth Leader of the Reich:

- German Young People for boys aged 10–13
- Young Girls for girls aged 10–14
- **Hitler Youth** for boys aged 14–18
- **League of German Maidens** for girls aged 14–18.

From 1936 membership was compulsory, although many did not join.

For the boys, the focus was on military training, sport, hiking and camping. The girls were kept separate from the boys. The main emphasis was on physical fitness and preparing them for motherhood through domestic skills. They were taught how to make beds and cook.

2.3 Successes and failures of Nazi policies

There were some successes:

- Membership of the Hitler Youth expanded from 5.4 million in 1936 to 7 million in 1939.
- Many young people enjoyed the exciting and interesting activities such as camping.
- Others enjoyed the great sense of comradeship and belonging to something that seemed powerful.

On other hand, there were failures:

- At least 3 million youngsters had not joined the Hitler Youth by the end of 1938.
- Some members found the activities boring, especially military drilling.

Key terms

Hitler Youth Organisation set up for boys in Germany to convert them to Nazi ideals

League of German Maidens Youth organisation for girls aged between 14 and 18 to prepare them for motherhood

Revision task

Summarise the differences in the experiences of girls and boys in Nazi Germany in education and youth movements.

Exam tip

Remember to focus on the different Nazi aims in their policies towards the young: for boys it was preparation for the military and for girls it was preparation for motherhood.

✏️ Utility

Look at the two sources, the exam-style question and the two answers below. Which answer is the better answer to the question and why? You could look at page 42 for guidance on how to answer the utility question to help you make your judgement.

How useful are Sources B and C for an enquiry into the Hitler Youth movement? Explain your answer, using Sources B and C and your own knowledge of the historical context.

SOURCE B

From a British magazine, 1938.

There seems little enthusiasm for the Hitler Youth, with membership falling. Many no longer want to be commanded, but wish to do as they like. Usually only a third of a group appears for roll-call. At evening meetings it is a great event if 20 turn up out of 80, but usually there are only about 10 or 12.

SOURCE C

A Nazi poster of 1936 for the League of German Maidens.

ANSWER 1

Source B is useful because it suggests that the Hitler Youth movement was not popular. At least 3 million youngsters had not joined the Hitler Youth by the end of 1938. It is also useful because it was from a British magazine which may well try to give a more objective and balanced view of life in the Hitler Youth.

Source C is useful because it provides an example of the propaganda used by the Nazis to encourage support for the Hitler Youth and more young people, in this case girls, to join. It is also useful because it provides evidence of the popularity of the movement as the girl looks happy and enthusiastic. Membership of the Hitler Youth certainly expanded from 5.4 million in 1936 to 7 million in 1939.

ANSWER 2

Source B is useful because it was written at the time. Source B is also useful because it tells me that there seems little enthusiasm for the Hitler Youth. It also says that only ten or twelve turn up for evening meetings.

Source C is useful because it is from the time of the Nazis. Source C is useful because it shows me a member of the League of German Maidens holding a Nazi flag. She has blonde hair. She is wearing a uniform.

3 Employment and living standards

Nazi policies reduced unemployment; however, there is debate about the standard of living during this period.

3.1 Nazi policies to reduce unemployment

Hitler was determined to reduce unemployment. This stood at 6 million in 1932 and had more or less been removed by 1938.

Job-creation schemes

In 1933, 18.4 billion marks were spent on job-creation schemes, rising to 37.1 million by 1938. One scheme was a massive road-building programme to create **autobahns**. This improved the efficiency of German industry by allowing goods to cross the country more quickly and enabled the swift transportation of German troops.

The Reich Labour Service (RAD)

The **Reich Labour Service** provided young men with manual labour jobs. From 1935, it was compulsory for men aged 18–25 to serve for six months. Workers lived in camps, wore uniforms, received very low pay and carried out military drill as well as work.

Invisible unemployment

Some unemployed people were 'invisible' and not counted in official unemployment figures:

- Jews dismissed from their jobs. From 1933, many Jews were forced out of their jobs, especially in the professions such as lawyers and doctors.
- Women doctors, civil servants and teachers dismissed from their jobs.
- Women who had given up work to get married.
- Unmarried men under 25 who were pushed into RAD schemes.
- Opponents of the regime held in concentration camps.

Rearmament

Rearmament, especially after 1936, created more jobs:

- More money was spent on manufacturing weapons, and other heavy industry grew, such as the iron industry. By 1939, 26 billion marks were spent on rearmament.
- From 1935, all men aged 18–35 had to do two years' military service. The army expanded from 100,000 in 1933 to 1,400,000 by 1939.

3.2 Changes in the standard of living

There is a debate about whether Germans were better or worse off during the period 1933–39.

Better off	Worse off
• There was more or less full employment. • The '**Strength Through Joy**' (KdF) tried to improve the leisure time of German workers through leisure and cultural trips. These included concerts, theatre visits, sporting events, weekend trips, holidays and cruises. • '**Beauty of Labour**' tried to improve working conditions. It organised the building of canteens, swimming pools and sports facilities. It installed better workplace lighting and improved noise levels.	• Lack of freedom. German workers lost their rights under the Nazis. In 1933, trade unions were banned (replaced by the **German Labour Front**). The Labour Front did not permit workers to negotiate for better pay or reduced hours of work. Strikes were banned. • Volkswagen swindle. This idea to encourage people to put aside money every week to buy a Volkswagen was a con trick. By 1939 not a single customer had taken delivery of a car. None of the money was refunded. • **Invisible unemployment**.

Key terms

Autobahns German motorways

Beauty of Labour A department of the KdF that tried to improve working conditions

German Labour Front An organisation of employers and workers which replaced trade unions

Invisible unemployment Unemployed people not included in the official unemployment statistics

Rearmament Building up the German armed forces

Reich Labour Service A scheme to provide young men with manual labour jobs

Strength Through Joy An organisation set up by the German Labour Front to try to improve the leisure time of German workers

Revision task

Rank order the various methods used by the Nazis to reduce unemployment beginning with the most effective and ending with the least effective.

Relevance

Below are an exam-style question and a series of statements. Decide which statements are:

- relevant to the question (R)
- partially relevant to the question (PR)
- irrelevant to the question (I).

Tick the appropriate column.

Explain why the Nazis were able to reduce unemployment in Germany in the years 1933–39.

> **You may use the following in your answer:**
> - **The National Labour Front**
> - **Job-creation schemes**
>
> You **must** also use information of your own.

Nazi policies	R	PR	I
In 1933, 18.4 billion marks were spent on job-creation schemes, rising to 37.1 million by 1938			
From 1933, more and more Jews were forced out of their jobs			
The Strength Through Joy movement organised leisure activities and provided the public with cheap holidays			
The Labour Front replaced trade unions. Workers were not allowed to leave their jobs without permission			
Germany had built a network of motorways, known as autobahns			
Beauty of Labour tried to improve working conditions by organising the building of canteens and sports facilities for workers			
The Reich Labour Service was made compulsory in July 1935 for all men aged 18–25, who had to serve six months			
The Depression brought unemployment which had reached 6 million by 1932			
Many women were dismissed from their jobs, especially in the professions. Others were tempted by marriage loans to give up their jobs and marry			
The RAD was not popular. Men were paid very low wages and had to put up with uncomfortable tented camps, long hours of work and boring jobs			
The drive for rearmament created more jobs as more money was spent on manufacturing weapons			
Billions were spent producing tanks, ships and aircraft. Heavy industry especially benefited			

 Better or worse?

1 Using the information on page 34, copy and complete both sides of the scales to show whether workers were better or worse off.

2 Do you think workers were better or worse off overall? Give reasons for your answer.

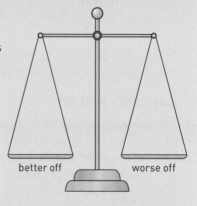

better off   worse off

4 The persecution of minorities

Hitler used the Jews as scapegoats for many of Germany's problems. The Nazis also persecuted **Slavs**, **Gypsies**, homosexuals and those with disabilities.

4.1 Nazi racial belief and policies

Central to the Nazis' policy was the aim to create a pure Aryan racial state. They thought this could be achieved by **selective breeding** and destroying the Jews. Jews and Slavs were seen as inferior *Untermenschen* or subhumans.

4.2 The treatment of minorities

Germans with disabilities were seen as a 'burden on the community'. There were also socially undesirable groups such as homosexuals and Gypsies.

People with disabilities

The 1933 Sterilisation Law allowed the sterilisation of those suffering from physical deformity, mental illness, epilepsy, learning disabilities, blindness and deafness.

Homosexuals

Homosexuality remained illegal. Nazi views about the importance of family life meant that same-sex relationships could not be tolerated. Gay men were arrested and sent to concentration camps.

Gypsies

The Nazis wanted to remove Germany's 30,000 Gypsies because they were non-Aryan and threatened racial purity. In 1935, the Nazis banned all marriages between Gypsies and Germans.

4.3 The persecution of the Jews

The persecution of the Jews gradually increased in the years 1933–39.

Early policies, 1933–34

- In 1933, the SA organised a boycott of Jewish shops and businesses.
- Jews were excluded from government jobs.
- In 1934, local councils banned Jews from public spaces such as parks.

The Nuremberg Laws, 1935

The Nuremberg Laws were a series of measures aimed against the Jews, including:

- The Reich Citizenship Law stated that only those of German blood could be German citizens. Jews lost their citizenship, and the right to vote and hold government office.
- The Law for the Protection of German Blood and Honour forbade marriage or sexual relations between Jews and German citizens.

Kristallnacht and after

On 8 November 1938, Goebbels organised anti-Jewish demonstrations which involved attacks on Jewish property, shops, homes and synagogues. So many windows were smashed that the events of 9 November 1938 became known as the 'Night of the Broken Glass' or **Kristallnacht**. Worse persecution of the Jews followed.

In January 1939, the SS was given the responsibility for eliminating Jews from Germany. This would be achieved by forced **emigration**:

- On 30 April, Jews were forced into **ghettos**.
- By the summer of 1939, about 250,000 Jews had left Germany.

Key terms

Emigration The act of leaving one's country to settle in another country

Ghettos Densely populated areas of a city inhabited by a particular ethnic group, such as Jews

Gypsy A race of people found across Europe who generally travel across the continent rather than living in one place

Kristallnacht The 'night of the broken glass'. The name given to a night of violence against Jews due to the amount of shattered glass which littered the streets

Nuremberg Laws Laws passed in 1935 which denied German citizenship to Jewish people

Selective breeding Nazi policy designed to create a master race

Slavs Eastern Europeans including Poles and Russians

Revision task

What were the following?

- The master race
- The Sterilisation Law of 1933
- The Nuremberg Laws
- Kristallnacht.

Exam tip

Remember that other minority groups apart from the Jews were persecuted by the Nazis.

You could get a question about how life for Jews changed in Nazi Germany 1933–39. It was a gradual build-up of Nazi policies against the Jews.

Making an inference from a visual source

An inference is a message that you can get from a source. Below are an exam-style inference question, the source and a series of statements. Decide which of the statements:

- make(s) inferences from the source (I)
- describes what can be seen in the source (D)
- cannot be justified from the source (X).

Give two things you can infer from Source A about the treatment of the Jews in Nazi Germany in the years 1936–39.

SOURCE A

A photograph taken in March 1933. It shows members of the SA forcing a Jewish lawyer to walk barefoot through the streets of Munich wearing a sign that says 'I will never again complain to the police'.

Statements	I	D	X
The photograph shows a Jewish man walking barefoot down a street			
Jewish shops were boycotted by the SA			
The Jews were treated unfairly			
The Jews were denied German citizenship			
The Jews were publicly humiliated			
Jewish shops and synagogues were destroyed by the Nazis			
The SA played a leading role in persecuting the Jews			
Members of the SA are forcing the Jewish man to walk down the street			

 You're the examiner

Below is an exam-style question.

Give two things you can infer about the treatment of the Jews in Nazi Germany.

1   Below are a mark scheme and a paragraph which is part of an answer to the question. Read the paragraph and the mark scheme. First decide which mark you would award the paragraph (there are a maximum of four marks available).

> **Mark scheme**
>
> Award 1 mark for each valid inference up to a maximum of two inferences. The second mark for each example should be awarded for supporting detail selected from the source.

The source suggests that the Jews in Nazi Germany were publicly humiliated. This is because the photograph shows a Jewish man being forced to walk down a main street barefooted. The source also suggests that the Jews had no protection from the police.

2   Next try and improve this answer to get four marks.

Exam focus

Your History GCSE is made up of three exams:

- Paper 1 on a thematic study and historic environment.
- Paper 2 on a British depth study and a period study.
- Paper 3 on a modern depth study, in your case Weimar and Nazi Germany, 1918–39.

For Paper 3 you have to answer the following types of questions. Each requires you to demonstrate different historical skills:

- **Question 1** is a source inference question in which you have to make two supported inferences.
- **Question 2** is a causation question which asks you to explain why something happened. You should develop at least three clear points.
- **Question 3** includes four sub-questions on an enquiry. For this enquiry you are given two sources and two interpretations.

The table below gives a summary of the question types for Paper 3 and what you need to do.

Question number	Marks	Key words	You need to...
1	4	Give **two** things you can infer from Source A about ...	• Make at least two inferences • Use quotes from the source to back up your inference, or describe a specific part of it if it is a picture
2	12	Explain why ... You may use the following in your answer: [two given points]. You **must** also use information of your own	• Explain at least three causes. You can use the points in the question but must also use at least one point of your own • Ensure that you focus these on the question
3(a)	8	How useful are sources ... for an enquiry into ... ?	• Ensure that you explain the value of the contents of each of the sources • Explain how the provenance of each source affects the value of the contents • You need to support your answer with your knowledge of the given topic
3(b)	4	Study Interpretations 1 and 2. What is the main difference between these views?	• Ensure that you understand the main view of each interpretation • Give the view from each interpretation to support your answer
3(c)	4	Suggest **one** reason why Interpretations 1 and 2 give different views	• Remember you only have to explain one reason • Make use of the two sources
3(d)	20	How far do you agree with Interpretation 2 about ... ?	• Ensure that you agree and disagree with the view • Use evidence from the interpretations and your own knowledge • Ensure that you write a conclusion giving your final judgement on the question • There are up to 4 marks for spelling, punctuation, grammar and the use of specialist terminology

Question 1: Inference

Below is an example of an exam-style inference question which is worth 4 marks.

Give two things you can infer from Source A about Hitler's meetings.

SOURCE A

Adapted from the diary of Luise Solmitz, 23 March 1932. Solmitz was a schoolteacher writing about attending a meeting in Hamburg at which Hitler spoke.

There stood Hitler in a simple black coat, looking over the crowd of 120,000 people of all classes and ages ... a forest of swastika flags unfurled, the joy of this moment showed itself in a roaring salute ... The crowd looked up to Hitler with touching faith, as their helper, their saviour, their deliverer from unbearable distress ... He is the rescuer of the scholar, the farmer, the worker and the unemployed.

Quick quizzes at **www.hoddereducation.co.uk/myrevisionnotes**

How to answer

You have to make two inferences and support each with details from the source. For each of the two inferences you are given the prompts 'What I can infer?' and 'Details in the source that tell me this'.

- **'What I can infer?'** Begin your answer with 'This source suggests …'. This should help you to get the message from the source.

- **'Details in the source that tell me this'** Then quote the detail from the source which supports this message. Begin this part of the answer with 'I know this because the source says/shows …'.

Below is a sample answer to this inference question with comments around it.

What I can infer:

The source suggests that Hitler appealed to many different sections in German society.

> The first inference is made. Using the phrase 'the source suggests' encourages this inference.

Details in the source that tell me this:

I know this because the source says 'He is the rescuer of the scholar, the farmer, the worker and the unemployed'.

> The first inference is supported with evidence from the source. This is reinforced by using the phrase 'I know this because'.

What I can infer:

The source also suggests the crowd were very enthusiastic about Hitler.

> The second inference is made. Using the phrase 'the source suggests' encourages this inference.

Details in the source that tell me this:

I know this because the source says 'the joy of this moment showed itself in a roaring salute … The crowd looked up to Hitler with touching faith'.

> The second inference is supported with evidence from the source. This is reinforced by using the phrase 'I know this because'.

Visual sources

You could also be asked to make inferences from a visual source.

Give two things you can infer from Source B about the police state.

Here is the first part of an answer to this question.

This source suggests that the police had a strong presence in Nazi Germany

I know this because the source shows several police with rifles who are thoroughly searching people in the street.

1 Highlight the following:
   - Where the student has made the inference.
   - How this inference has been supported.
2 Now add a second supported inference.

SOURCE B

German citizens being searched in the street by Gestapo officers and armed uniformed police, 1933.

Question 2: Causation

Below is an example of an exam-style causation question which is worth 12 marks.

Explain why the Weimar Republic experienced a period of recovery, 1923–29.

> **You may use the following in your answer:**
> ■ The Dawes Plan   ■ The Locarno Pact
> **You must also use information of your own.**

How to answer

● You need to explain at least three causes. This could be the two mentioned in the question and one of your own. You don't have to use the points given in the question, you could decide to make more points of your own instead.

● You need to fully explain each cause and support your explanation with precise knowledge, ensuring that each cause is fully focused on the question.

Below is a sample answer to this question with comments around it.

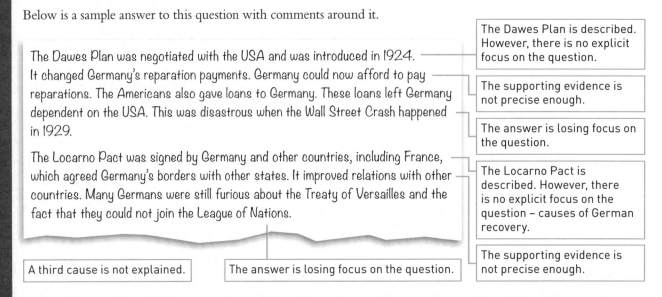

The Dawes Plan was negotiated with the USA and was introduced in 1924. It changed Germany's reparation payments. Germany could now afford to pay reparations. The Americans also gave loans to Germany. These loans left Germany dependent on the USA. This was disastrous when the Wall Street Crash happened in 1929.

The Locarno Pact was signed by Germany and other countries, including France, which agreed Germany's borders with other states. It improved relations with other countries. Many Germans were still furious about the Treaty of Versailles and the fact that they could not join the League of Nations.

> The Dawes Plan is described. However, there is no explicit focus on the question.

> The supporting evidence is not precise enough.

> The answer is losing focus on the question.

> The Locarno Pact is described. However, there is no explicit focus on the question – causes of German recovery.

> The supporting evidence is not precise enough.

> A third cause is not explained.

> The answer is losing focus on the question.

 Make an improvement

Try improving the answer. An example of a better answer to this question is on page 41 for you to check your own answer against.

> **Exam tip**
>
> Writing a good paragraph to explain an answer to something is as easy as **PEE**ing – Point, Example, Explain.
>
> Your point is a short answer to the question. You then back this up with lots of examples to demonstrate all the knowledge you have learned during your studies: this is the section that proves you have studied and revised, rather than just
>
> guessing. Finally, you will link that knowledge to the question by explaining in a final sentence:
> ● **P**oint: passing my GCSE History exam will be very helpful in the future.
> ● **E**xample: for example, it will help me to continue my studies next year.
> ● **E**xplain: this will help me to get the job I want in the future.

Below is a sample answer to the causation question on page 40 with comments around it.

A first cause of German recovery was the Dawes Plan of 1924. This was because this plan reorganised Germany's reparation payments and encouraged further financial support from the USA. German reparations were not reduced but more sensibly staged to match Germany's capacity to pay. Reparations would begin at 1 billion marks for the first year, and would increase over a period of four to five years to 2.5 billion marks. Thereafter, the payments would be linked to Germany's capacity to pay. In return, the French withdrew their troops from the Ruhr. Furthermore, the Dawes Plan included a US loan of 800 million gold marks to Germany. Over the next six years Germany borrowed about $3 billion from US companies and banks, which greatly assisted the growth of German industry as well as the payment of reparations.

> The first cause is introduced and immediately focuses on the question.

> The supporting evidence is precise and relevant to the question.

However, the success of the Dawes Plan was closely linked to a second reason for German recovery, the Rentenmark, which provided the financial stability necessary for economic recovery. The German currency had lost all value due to the hyperinflation of 1923. In November 1923, Stresemann, in order to stabilise the currency, introduced this new currency. This was a temporary measure with its value based on property values. In the following year, the Rentenmark was converted into the Reichsmark, a new currency now backed with gold.

> The second cause is introduced and linked to the first cause and immediately focuses on the question. Notice that this is a cause not mentioned in the question.

> The supporting evidence is precise and relevant to the question.

Economic and financial recovery was supported by improved relations abroad, which was a third reason for recovery. Stresemann greatly improved relations with Britain and France by ending passive resistance in the Ruhr and signing the Locarno Pact of 1925. The Pact also included Italy and Belgium and guaranteed Germany's frontiers with France, Belgium and Italy. In the following year, Stresemann took Germany into the League of Nations. Germany was recognised as a Great Power and given a permanent seat on the League's council alongside France and Britain. This, in turn, encouraged further trade between these countries and greater economic investment in Germany.

> The third cause is introduced and linked to the second cause and immediately focuses on the question.

> The supporting evidence is precise and relevant to the question.

 Have a go

Now have a go at the following causation question:

Explain why there was increased support for the Nazis in the years 1919–32.

You may use the following in your answer:
- Hitler
- Fear of Communism

You **must** also use information of your own.

Question 3(a): Utility

Below is an example of an exam-style utility question. It is worth 8 marks.

How useful are Sources B and C for an enquiry into Nazi policies towards women in Germany in the years 1933–39?

SOURCE B

From Judith Grunfeld, an American journalist, 1937.

How many women workers did the Führer send home? According to the statistics of the German Department of Labour, there were in June 1936, 5,470,000 employed women, or 1,200,000 more than in January 1933. The Nazi campaign has not been successful in reducing the numbers of women employed. It has simply squeezed them out of better paid positions into the sweated trades. This type of labour with its miserable wages and long hours is extremely dangerous to the health of women and degrades the family.

SOURCE C

A Nazi poster of 1934 which says 'the NSDAP [Nazi Party] protects the national community'.

How to answer

- Explain the value and limitations of the contents of each source and try to add some contextual knowledge when you make a point.
- Explain the value and limitations of the NOP (Nature, Origin and Purpose) of each source and try to add some contextual knowledge when you make a point.

- In your conclusion, give a final judgement on the relative value of each source. For example, one source might provide one view of an event, the other source a different view.

Quick quizzes at **www.hoddereducation.co.uk/myrevisionnotes**

1 Below are a mark scheme and a paragraph which is part of an answer to the question on page 42.
Read the paragraph and the mark scheme. Decide which level you would award the paragraph. Give a
justification for your choice.

Mark scheme		
Level	**Mark**	
1	1–2	A simple judgement on utility is given, and supported by undeveloped comment on the content of the sources and/or their provenance
2	3–5	Judgements on source utility for the specified enquiry are given ... related to the content of the sources and/or their provenance
3	6–8	Judgements on source utility for the specified enquiry are given ... with developed reasoning which takes into account how the provenance affects the usefulness of the source content

Source B is useful because it suggests that the Nazi policies towards women were not successful
as there were 1,200,000 more women in employment in Germany in 1936 than there had been
in 1933. This was the case because there were labour shortages in certain parts of German
industry. It is also useful because it says that the Nazi policies had not been successful because
they had forced women out of reasonably paid jobs into those that had poor conditions such as
the sweated trades. Source B is also useful because it was written in 1937.

Source C is useful because it suggests that women in Nazi Germany played an important role in
the family. The poster shows the woman in the very centre holding and looking after the baby. The
Nazis were keen on ensuring that women did all the household duties. It is also useful because it is
a Nazi poster which was produced in 1934.

Level ☐   Reason _____

_____

Below is part of a high-level answer to the question on page 42 which explains the utility of Source B.
Read it and the comments around it.

Source B is useful because it suggests that the Nazi policies towards women
were not successful as there were 1,200,000 more women in employment
in Germany in 1936 than there had been in 1933. This was the case because
there were labour shortages in certain parts of German industry. It is also useful
because it says that the Nazi policies had not been successful because they had
forced women out of reasonably paid jobs into those that had poor conditions
such as the sweated trades. 'Invisible employment' enabled the Nazis to hide the
real extent of unemployment. The usefulness of Source B is further enhanced
by its provenance. It was written by an American journalist who will not have
been influenced by Nazi propaganda and censorship and would be able to give
an objective, independent assessment of the effects of Nazi policies on women.
She is able to be critical about these policies.

> A judgement is made on the value of the contents of the source.

> Own knowledge is used to support this judgement.

> The provenance of the source is taken into account when making a judgement on its utility.

2 Now write your own high-level answer on Source C. Remember to take into account how the
provenance affects the usefulness of the source content.

Question 3(b): How interpretations differ

Below is an example of an exam-style question 3(b) on the difference between two interpretations. It is worth 4 marks.

Study Interpretations 1 and 2. They give different views of Nazi policies towards women in the years 1933–39. What is the main difference between these views? Explain your answer, using details from both interpretations.

INTERPRETATION 1

From Germany 1918–45 *by J. Brooman, published in 1996.*

Women were soon brought in line. Shortly after the Nazi seizure of power, thousands of married women doctors and civil servants were sacked from their jobs. Over the next few years, the number of women teachers was gradually reduced. From 1936 onwards women could no longer be judges or prosecutors, nor could they serve on juries.

INTERPRETATION 2

From Weimar and Nazi Germany *by E. Wilmot, published in 1993.*

In 1933 there were 4.85 million women in paid employment. This increased to 7.14 million in 1939. Economic reality forced Nazi ideology to do a U-turn. A labour shortage began to develop from 1936 and the government looked to women to plug the gap. In 1937, the Nazis overturned a clause in the marriage loans scheme to permit married women who had a loan to take up employment.

How to answer

You need to identify the main view that each interpretation has about the Nazi policies towards women in the years 1933–39 and explain each view. Below is an answer to this question which explains how the interpretations differ.

Question 3(c): Why interpretations differ

A main difference is that Interpretation 1 emphasises the success of Nazi policies towards women in Germany in the years 1933–39, especially in removing married women from employment. Interpretation 2 emphasises the failure of Nazis policies towards women in Germany in the years 1933–39, especially in employment – with more women in employment by 1939.

> The main view of Interpretation 1 is identified and explained.

> The main view of Interpretation 2 is identified and explained.

Below is an example of question 3(c) on the reasons why the two interpretations differ. It is worth 4 marks.

Suggest one reason why Interpretations 1 and 2 give different views about the achievements of Nazi policies towards women in the years 1933–39. You may use Sources B and C (see page 42) to help explain your answer.

How to answer

There are three reasons as to why the two interpretations differ. You only need to give one of these.

- The interpretations may differ because they have given weight to the two different sources. You need to identify the views given in the two sources and match these to the different interpretations.

- The interpretations may differ because they are partial extracts and in this case they do not actually contradict one another.
- They may differ because the authors have a different emphasis.

Below is part of an answer to this question in which the student uses the first option – they give different weight to different sources.

The interpretations may differ because they give different weight to different sources. For example, Source B provides some support for Interpretation 1, which stresses the failure of Nazi policies in removing women from employment.

> Interpretation 1 is matched to Source B.

> The view given in Source C is explained.

Have a go

Now, on a separate piece of paper, complete this answer by matching Interpretation 2 to one of the sources.

Question 3(d): How far do you agree with one of the interpretations?

Below is an example of an exam-style question 3(d) which asks you to make a judgement about how far you agree with one of the interpretations. It is worth 20 marks.

How far do you agree with Interpretation 2 about Nazi policies towards women in the years 1933–39? Explain your answer, using both interpretations and your knowledge of the historical context.

How to answer

You need to give a balanced answer which agrees and disagrees with the interpretation using evidence from the two interpretations as well as your own knowledge. Here is one way you could approach this:

- agree with the view with evidence from Interpretation 2
- agree with the view with evidence from your own knowledge
- disagree with the view with evidence from Interpretation 1

- disagree with the view with evidence from your own knowledge
- make a final judgement on the view.

Below is part of an answer to this question in which the student agrees with the view given in Interpretation 2.

I agree with the view given in Interpretation 2 about the achievements of Nazi policies towards women in the years 1933–39. The interpretation suggests that these policies, especially in the area of employment, were not successful. The Nazis' original aim was to remove as many women as possible from the work force to help with their other policy of reducing unemployment and also to ensure that married women could focus on their domestic role as wives and mothers.

> The answer immediately focuses on the question.

> Support is provided from Interpretation 2 for this view.

However, as Wilmot suggests, the Nazis had to do a U-turn in the mid-1930s as there were labour shortages so that the number of women employed actually increased from 4.85 million in 1933 to 7.14 million in 1939. In addition, the numbers increased because many employers preferred women workers as they were cheaper. Women's wages remained only two-thirds of men's. The Nazis did force women out of the better paid and more professional jobs. However, more and more employed women were employed in lower paid jobs with poor working conditions such as the sweated trades. Some women resented the loss of these more professional jobs such as doctors, lawyers and schoolteachers.

> Own knowledge is used to provide support for the view.

Have a go

Now, on a separate piece of paper, have a go at writing the rest of the answer by disagreeing with the view given in Interpretation 2.

Remember to write a conclusion giving your final judgement on the question. Here is an example of a good conclusion.

Overall, I only partly agree with Interpretation 2 about Nazi policies towards women. As suggested by Wilmot, the Nazis did eventually have to change their employment policies and allow more women to work in industry. However, as Brooman suggests in Interpretation 1, the Nazis did achieve one of their aims in female employment which was to reduce the number of women in professional jobs.

Revision techniques

HOW CAN I REMEMBER IT ALL ?

We all learn in different ways and if you're going to be successful in your revision you need to work out the ways that work best for you. Remember that revision doesn't have to be dull and last for hours at a time – but it is really important you do it! The highest grades are awarded to students who have consistently excellent subject knowledge and this only comes with solid revision.

Method 1: 'Brain dumps'

These are particularly useful when done every so often – it's never too early to start! Take a big piece of paper or even a whiteboard and write down everything you can remember about the topic you are revising, one of the units or even the whole History course. You could write down:

- dates
- names of key individuals
- key events
- important place names
- anything else you can remember.

Once you're satisfied you can't remember any more, use different colours to highlight or underline the words in groups. For example, you might choose to underline all the mentions that relate to causes of the Depression in Germany in 1929 in red and effects in blue.

You could extend this task by comparing your brain dump with that of a friend. The next time you do it, try setting yourself a shorter time limit and see if you can write down more.

Method 2: Learning walks

Make use of your space! Write down key facts and place them around your home, where you will see them every day. Make an effort to read the facts whenever you walk past them. You might decide to put information on Hitler's rise to power on the stairs, with the idea of steadily achieving his dictatorship.

Studies have shown that identifying certain facts with a certain place can help them stick in your mind. So, when you get into the exam room and you find you have a question on the recovery of the Weimar Republic, 1924–29, you can close your eyes and picture that factsheet on your living-room wall … what does it say?

Method 3: 'Distilling'

Memory studies show that we retain information better if we revisit it regularly. This means that revising the information once is not necessarily going to help it stay in your brain. Going back over the facts at intervals of less than a week leads to the highest retention of facts.

To make this process streamlined, try 'distilling' your notes. Start by reading over the notes you've completed in class or in this revision guide; two days later, read over them again, and this time write down everything you didn't remember. If you repeat this process enough you will end up with hardly any facts left to write down, because they will all be stored in your brain, ready for the exam!

Method 4: Using your downtime

There are always little pockets of time through the day which aren't much good for anything: bus journeys, queues, ad breaks in TV programmes, waiting for the bath to run and so on. If you added all these minutes up it would probably amount to quite a lot of time, and it can be put to good use for revision.

Instead of having to carry around your notes, though, make use of something you carry around with you already. Most of us have a phone that can take pictures and record voice memos, or an iPod or something similar:

- Photograph key sections of this book and read over them.
- Record yourself reading information so that you can listen back over it – while you're playing football, before you go to sleep, or at any other time.
- Access the quizzes that go with this book: www.hoddereducation.co.uk/myrevisionnotes